SEA TURTLES

Ocean Nomads

BY

MARY M. CERULLO

PHOTOGRAPHS BY

JEFFREY L. ROTMAN

DUTTON CHILDREN'S BOOKS • NEW YORK

To Jeannie Meggison, who has brought her love of the sea to thousands of schoolchildren —M.M.C.

To Matthew and Thomas —J.L.R.

Thank you to Guy Ayalon, Director of Underwater Observatory Marine Park, Eilat, Israel, for allowing me to photograph and observe his conservation efforts in repopulating sea turtles of the Red Sea; Sherri Floyd, Connie Merigo, and especially Kathy Streeter of the New England Aquarium, Boston, Massachusetts; and to Mike Engeman, turtle aficionado

Library of Congress Cataloging-in-Publication Data

Cerullo, Mary M.

Sea turtles: ocean nomads / Mary M. Cerullo; photographs by Jeffrey L. Rotman.—lst ed.

p.   cm.

Summary : Presents information on the physical characteristics, behavior, habitat, various species, and life cycle of sea turtles, along with a discussion of their endangered status and the efforts being made to study and conserve them.

ISBN 0-525-46649-5

1. Sea turtles—Juvenile literature. [1. Sea turtles. 2. Turtles. 3. Endangered species.]

I. Rotman, Jeffrey L., ill. II. Title.

QL666.C536 C38 2003   597.92'8—dc21   2002074150

Published in the United States by Dutton Children's Books,

a division of Penguin Young Readers Group

345 Hudson Street, New York, New York 10014

www.penguin.com

Designed by Heather Wood

First Edition

Manufactured in China

5 7 9 10 8 6 4

Title-page photograph:
Newborn hawksbill turtle, at night, Sipadan Island

CONTENTS

3

CHAPTER ONE

Sea Turtle Island

Barely rising above the horizon, a tropical island sits alone in a turquoise sea. It is Sipadan Island, a tiny speck in the western Pacific Ocean, a hundred miles off the coast of Borneo. This remote outpost is the destination of divers Jeff Rotman and Marcello Bertinetti and, not coincidentally, two endangered species of sea turtles. The men came here just to meet these sea turtles.

Sipadan Island was formed from a coral reef that grew around the slopes of an extinct underwater volcano. Limestone caves riddle the coral reef, creating long, dark passages. These caves were the location that Jeff and Marcello had chosen for their first dive. To reach the entrance, they swam a short way down a steep coral wall that plunged six thousand feet to the ocean floor. Brightly colored sea fans and sponges hugged the vertical slope. A parrot fish munching on coral ignored them as they drifted past. The divers found the entrance to the coral cave thirty feet below the surface. The two men squeezed into the narrow crevice just as a school of silvery barracuda flashed by.

Islanders had warned the divers that they easily

Above: *A green sea turtle swims toward shore where she will lay her eggs.*
Opposite: *Sipadan Island is an outpost for sea turtles and divers in the tropical Pacific Ocean.*

could become lost in the maze of tunnels of underwater caves. As the tight passageway opened into a huge chamber, Jeff's dive light revealed that earlier visitors to this cave had met just such a fate. More than a dozen sea-turtle skeletons were strewn across the cavern floor. A turtle that had recently died floated against the ceiling. No wonder the locals call this place the "Turtle Tomb."

CREATURES OF THE CORAL REEF

The coral reef has been compared to an underwater city, with many different animals crowded into crevices like high-rise apartment dwellers. The coral reef provides food, protection, and mates for its many residents and visitors. Coral reefs are home to a quarter of all the oceans' species, including about 3,500 species of fish and 600 species of reef-building corals. Reef-building corals thrive on the eastern shores of large landmasses like Australia and Indonesia, around small islands like those in the Caribbean Sea, and in tropical waters like the Red Sea and the Indian Ocean. No place else on earth, except possibly the rain forest, can match a coral reef for its variety of creatures. Reef-building corals ("hard corals") and sea fans ("soft corals") come in many vibrant colors, as do the reef fishes themselves. Schools of barracuda patrol the reef in search of colorful residents like parrot fish, butterfly fish, and angelfish. Parrot fish, with teeth that have fused together to make a strong, beaklike scraper, grind up chunks of coral to feed on the tiny plants living within.

Below: *Coral reef with Sergeant Major and Scissortail Sergeant, Red Sea, Egypt*
Opposite: *Scalefin anthias schooling on coral reef in the Red Sea*

A diver examines the remains of a sea turtle lost in the maze of underwater caves.

The bones of green sea turtles and hawksbill turtles littered the cave. The scene made the divers think of the legendary elephant graveyards of Africa, where elephants go to die. But these turtles had not come here intending to die. They had almost certainly wandered into the caves in search of food or a quiet spot to take a nap. Then they had become confused by the warren of tunnels and couldn't find their way out again.

Like humans, sea turtles breathe air. They usually stay submerged for four or five minutes at a time and can hold their breath for several hours when they are sleeping. But they use up oxygen quickly if they panic, as they might if they were caught in a fisherman's net or lost in a labyrinth of caves. How long they survived in Turtle Tomb is anyone's guess.

Once they died, their bodies were attacked by shrimp, crabs, and worms. Only their skeletons (of which their shell is part) were left behind. As the divers gazed at the remains of the stranded sea turtles before them, they felt a sudden urge to check their air supply.

Jeff and Marcello had come to Sipadan Island to photograph the sea turtles whose ancestors had nested here undisturbed for countless generations. The men were concerned that this remote island was fast becoming a popular attraction for divers who came in ever increasing numbers to watch the sea turtles mate and lay their eggs. Would the resorts, dive shops, and marinas that were being built for the tourists drive away the very thing they were all coming to see? Fortunately, Jeff and Marcello also found island game wardens working to make sure Sipadan Island would continue to welcome both human and turtle visitors. The changes happening on this tiny island made underwater photographer Jeff Rotman want to learn how sea turtles were being threatened, and protected, around the world.

SEA TURTLES FACE A SEA OF DANGERS

A diver tries to photograph a shy green sea turtle.

Sea turtles face many more dangers than becoming lost in a submarine cave. Almost all those perils can be traced back to humans. Sea turtles have been killed for their meat and shells, drowned in fishing nets, run over by ships, or suffocated after mistakenly eating plastic bags, balloons, Styrofoam, and other plastic garbage. Thousands of turtles are drowned each year after being accidentally caught in shrimp-fishing nets. Others become entangled in plastic nets, lines, and buoys either lost by fishermen or set out for other prey, such as sharks or swordfish. Oil spills can pollute the breeding or feeding grounds of sea turtles. Tar balls can carry oil-spill damage far across the ocean. Tar can coat the eyes, nostrils, and mouths of the unfortunate sea turtles that encounter it.

A game warden checks on a hawksbill turtle nest.

CHAPTER TWO

Seaworthy Turtles

All turtles are reptiles, the same as snakes, lizards, and geckos. They are cold-blooded animals, which means they take on the temperature of their surroundings. Reptiles all have scaly, dry skin, but turtles also have shells. The top shell (the *carapace*) and the bottom shell (the *plastron*) are actually part of their skeleton. The scales covering both shells, called *scutes*, are made of keratin, the same material as human fingernails.

Instead of teeth, turtles have jagged beaks for catching, holding, and slicing their food.

Their nostrils and eyes are located near the top of the head so a turtle doesn't have to stick its head far out of the water to breathe. Scientists believe sea turtles can see better underwater than on land. Out of water they become rather nearsighted. Their sense of smell is excellent. Turtles have no external ears, but they can hear.

11

A sea turtle has to lift its head only slightly above water to breathe. A green turtle in sea fan coral, Grand Cayman.

TURTLE HEARING TEST

Just how well turtles hear is the subject of an experiment using Myrtle the Turtle, a 550-pound green sea turtle that has lived at the New England Aquarium in Massachusetts for over thirty years. Myrtle is used to being fed by hand. Scuba divers enter the Giant Ocean Tank five times a day to feed the tropical fish, sharks, and sea turtles that live in the 200,000-gallon aquarium. As soon as the divers enter the tank, Myrtle is at their side nuzzling them for handouts. Because she has spent most of her life in human company, she enjoys interacting with humans. Comments one of her caregivers, Senior Aquarist Sherri Floyd, "She follows the divers around the tank and watches whatever they are doing. She loves to have

her back scratched, and she'll fall asleep in your lap."

Because Myrtle is exceptionally friendly and curious, she was the perfect subject for studying the hearing ability of sea turtles. Curator Kathy Streeter is teaching Myrtle to take a hearing test much like the ones given to human children. Myrtle is given various sounds of differing loudness to determine her hearing range. In the experiment, two speakers are lowered into the water. When Myrtle hears a sound, she pecks at a response paddle and gets a reward of squid. Kathy said, "So far it has been determined that Myrtle hears between 100–500 Hz. This is a smaller range of hearing than humans but includes some frequencies that are below our range of hearing." Loud sounds drive her away from the speakers, however.

Kathy has nothing but admiration for Myrtle's ability to master the complex series of procedures that have enabled researchers to measure Myrtle's hearing. Kathy tried several different procedures until she found the one that was easiest for Myrtle to respond to consistently. Myrtle also has to ignore the distraction of the other residents in her tank and the human visitors that crowd around its windows. Kathy notes that despite these challenges, "It is amazing that an animal with such a small brain has been able to learn the procedure required to participate in a hearing study!"

Scientists hope this study will help them understand how undersea noise pollution, from propeller-driven ship engines, drilling for oil on the ocean floor, and even scientific sonar studies, may affect sea turtles. Also, they hope that noise levels that annoy Myrtle can someday be broadcast from fishing boats to drive away sea turtles before they become entangled in fishing nets. This could help prevent one of the major causes of turtle deaths.

Myrtle the Turtle, a longtime resident of the New England Aquarium, is the subject of a study to find out how well turtles hear.

Broad flippers help sea turtles scull through the water. Hawksbill turtle.

Streamlined shells and paddle-shaped flippers help make sea turtles excellent swimmers and impressive divers. Leatherback sea turtles, for example, regularly dive deeper than 1,000 feet and have been known to reach a depth of 3,900 feet. The green sea turtle can hold its breath for as long as five hours, slowing its heart rate to as little as nine beats a minute to conserve oxygen. Some sea turtles have even been found to hibernate on the bottom, much as pond turtles do. Off the coast of California, black sea turtles bury themselves in mud or sand and remain dormant from November to March.

The buoyancy of seawater, which allows ships weighing hundreds of tons to float, also enables sea turtles to grow huge compared to most land turtles. Sea turtles range in size from the ridley, the smallest at about eighty pounds, to the leatherback, the largest at well over one thousand pounds. Streamlined and graceful in the ocean, bulky sea turtles become slow and clumsy on land.

Most sea turtles live in warm climates. If a sea turtle ventures into colder water, either swept by currents or by storms or searching for food, it may become "cold-stunned." At first, it loses the ability to swim, drifting helplessly at the surface of the water. Eventually, it becomes dazed and unresponsive, like a hiker lost in a snowstorm. If it is to survive, rescuers must warm the turtle up gradually, which may take

There are many differences between freshwater turtles, which you might find in ponds and pet stores, and sea turtles. A pond turtle has flat feet, webbed toes for swimming, and sharp claws for digging in the mud and for courting when the male uses its claws to tickle the female under the chin. A sea turtle's feet are broad flippers that are just used for swimming. A pond turtle can bend its neck into an S-shape to pull its head inside its shell, but a sea turtle cannot.

A leatherback sea turtle

several days to a week, and force-feed it to keep it alive.

Only the leatherback turtle seems to be able to handle the cold. It is the only species of sea turtles known to be active in water below 40°F. Leatherbacks have been seen as far north as Nova Scotia in Canada and Norway in northern Europe. A thick, oily fat layer under their skin helps them keep their body temperature warmer than the surrounding seawater. They also have the ability to divert blood flow away from their flippers and pump it to warm vital organs like the heart and brain.

SPECIES OF SEA TURTLES

Some scientists say there are eight species of sea turtles; others claim there are only seven. Since classification is a human invention, it makes no difference to the turtles. Most species of sea turtles were named for some distinctive feature, like the hawksbill turtle (*Eretmochelys imbricata*), which gets its name from its sharp, birdlike beak.

The hawksbill is the most tropical of sea turtles. It hangs out in coral reefs and rocky shorelines, wedging itself between rocks or coral crevices to nap. It can poke its sharp snout into small openings in the coral reef to seize shrimp, sponges, anemones, and squid. Small for a sea turtle, it usually only grows to about three feet long and weighs up to 150 pounds. But it lays more eggs than any other sea turtle—150 or more at one time.

The downfall of the hawksbill turtle is its shell. The overlapping plates, or scutes, of its top shell are thick, strong, and beautifully patterned, making it ideal for fashioning into tortoiseshell jewelry, eyeglass frames, and combs. Because of the popularity of "tortoiseshell" souvenirs, most of which were made in Japan, hawksbill turtle populations declined by 80 percent until international trade was stopped in 1982.

The most noticeable feature of the loggerhead turtle (*Caretta caretta*) is its bulging head, but it can also be identified by its enormous heart-shaped shell. This sea turtle dines on a wide variety of prey, including shellfish, horseshoe crabs, green crabs, clams, mussels, and shrimp as well as fish, sea urchins, squid, and jellyfish. It nests along the southeastern coast of the United States, particularly Florida, and on one island in Oman in the Middle East.

The flatback turtle (*Nataron depressus*) was named for its very flat shell. It lives along the coast of northern Australia and is a common sight in coastal coral reefs and grassy shallows, especially around the Great Barrier Reef. Adults may weigh as much as 198 pounds and grow to 39 inches long. Female flatbacks lay about fifty eggs at a time, but they are bigger than many other kinds of sea-turtle eggs, and so are their hatchlings.

16

The leatherback sea turtle (*Dermochelys coriacea*) is named for its soft, rubbery shell that looks like leather. The champion of sea turtles, it dives the deepest, travels the farthest, and grows the biggest. The largest leatherback was almost ten feet long from its beak to its tail and weighed over two thousand pounds. Its primary food is jellyfish. Jellyfish are 90 percent water, which doesn't seem a hearty enough meal to support an animal this size, but leatherbacks seem to eat enough to get by. Young leatherbacks in captivity often devour twice their weight in jellyfish each day. In their quest for jellyfish, leatherbacks sometimes mistakenly swallow floating garbage such as plastic milk jugs, Styrofoam, plastic bags, and balloons. This plastic debris can choke them or block food from passing through their digestive systems, causing them to slowly starve to death.

Some sea turtles are named for the color of their shells, like the black turtle that has a black shell. Some scientists think the black turtle (*Chelonia agassizii*) should be lumped in the same group as the green turtle. It ranges across the eastern Pacific Ocean and grows to 100 to 150 pounds. It is found in the tropical regions of the Pacific and Indian Oceans and in the southern and eastern parts of the Atlantic Ocean.

The olive ridley (*Lepidochelys olivacea*) is a small, olive-green turtle that feeds in shallow water on crabs, young spiny lobsters, and snails. It lives in tropical waters in the Atlantic, Pacific, and Indian Oceans. Olive ridleys are thought to be the most abundant sea turtles.

The shell of the green turtle (*Chelonia mydas*) is not green, but the fat just under its carapace is. That's because as an adult it is a vegetarian that feeds mostly on sea grass and seaweeds. Turtle soup made from this fatty layer became a favorite of wealthy Londoners in the 1800s. Lewis Carroll even wrote of it in *Alice in Wonderland:*

Beautiful Soup, so rich and green,
Waiting in a hot tureen!
Who for such dainties would not stoop?
Soup of the evening, beautiful Soup!
Soup of the evening, beautiful Soup!

One turtle was named for its "discoverer." The Kemp's ridley (*Lepidochelys kempii*) was named in 1880 for Richard Kemp, a fisherman who shipped turtles to Harvard University from Key West in Florida. It is the most endangered, and the smallest, of all sea turtles. Adults grow slightly over two feet long and weigh up to a hundred pounds. Adult Kemp's ridleys travel throughout the Gulf of Mexico, yet they are rarely found in nearby Caribbean waters. A few drift northward along the Atlantic coast and even cross over to Europe.

The females crawl up onto the shore together and lay their eggs in huge mass nestings called *arribadas* (Spanish for "the arrival"). Bands of mothers swarm up the beach at regular intervals from April to June each year. Unlike most other sea turtles, their invasion takes place during the daytime. That was lucky for engineer Andrés Herrera, the first person to ever film the nesting site of the Kemp's ridleys over half a century ago. He flew along the Gulf coast of Mexico for twenty-five days in a row until finally he discovered more than forty thousand sea turtles massed on a small strip of beach in Rancho Nuevo, Mexico. Although their numbers are on the rise, at one time as few as four hundred Kemp's ridleys nested there.

page 16: *The head of a hawksbill turtle resembles a bird's beak.*
page 17: *The flesh of the green turtle is green because it normally feeds on sea lettuce and seaweeds.*
Below: *Most sea turtles, like this hawksbill turtle, frequent the warm ocean waters around a coral reef.*

18

CHAPTER THREE

Time on Land

A sea turtle's time on land is short but crucial—and very dangerous.

A TOUGH CHILDHOOD

The first few days of a sea turtle's life are the most perilous. A tiny hawksbill turtle getting ready to hatch from its nest on Sipadan Island on a warm October night illustrates what baby turtles have to go through. After two months under the sand, it cracks out of its shell using a small knob on its head called an *egg tooth*. It stays hidden under the sand for a few more nights as about one hundred siblings hatch all around it. Then they all begin digging frantically for the surface. They emerge at the same time, in darkness. Their cue, apparently, is the cooling of the sand after the sun has set.

Once they are on the surface, the hatchlings are attracted to the light on the ocean's horizon and repelled by the darkness of the towering sand dunes. Together they race toward the sea, flailing the sand with their oarlike flippers.

Suddenly the air is filled with the flap of wings and the screech of seabirds. Birds, along with coconut crabs and lizards, carry off dozens of tiny turtles before they can reach the sea. Some of the silver-dollar-sized hatchlings fall into footprints in the sand, trapping them until predators find them. A few head in the wrong direction, toward the lights of new buildings behind the dunes. Some make it to

Newly hatched sea turtles instinctively head toward the ocean.

the shoreline where the waves scoop them up and carry them beyond the reach of land predators but into the path of fish waiting just offshore.

How many will survive? The chances of a hatchling ever making it to maturity are about one in one thousand. If even a few hatchlings live long enough to return to this beach twenty-five years later and lay eggs themselves, that is enough to renew the population.

MOTHER AT WORK

Only a few yards away from the stampeding hatchlings on Sipadan Island, a female green sea turtle crawls out of the surf onto the beach. Although she was agile under the sea, her 300-pound bulk makes her slow and clumsy on land. She moves by lifting her body up onto her two front flippers and shoving herself forward with the rear ones. Tears stream down her face, removing excess salt and clearing her eyes of sand. Her heavy top shell presses the thinner

WILL I BE A GIRL OR A BOY?

For several species of sea turtles, perhaps all, the temperature of the sand that surrounds the nest determines if the turtles will become male or female. Warm temperatures turn out females; cooler temperatures produce males. Egg nests that are buried deep in the sand or under shady trees tend to have a higher percentage of males, while nests baking under the hot sun tend to produce females. Where the egg is located in the nest may also decide its sex—eggs in the center (where it's warmer) may turn out to be females, while those on the cooler outer edges of the nest may become

males. Even the time of the year can make a difference. In Costa Rica, eggs that hatched in December and January during the cooler, rainy season were mostly males, while eggs laid in April and November turned out mostly female. (How can you tell the sex of a sea turtle? It's not easy. It's not until they mature that you can tell the difference, when the claws and tails of males grow significantly longer than those of females'.)

Above: *Male turtles have long tails; female turtles have short ones.*
Opposite: *A newborn hawksbill turtle escapes to the sea*

bottom shell against her lungs, making it hard for her to breathe. Her struggle can be heard in her short, puffy snorts.

She labors up the beach beyond the high-tide line, past where seawater could kill her developing eggs. Once she chooses a suitable spot, she begins to dig. She uses all her flippers to make a depression large enough to cradle her body. Then she uses her back flippers to scoop out the sand to make a bottle-shaped hole. She drops several slippery eggs into the hole, rests briefly, and continues. In the space of an hour, she deposits about 115 leathery eggs the size of Ping-Pong balls into the nest. Then she uses her hind flippers to fill in the hole. She carefully packs the sand with her rear flippers, and finally she shovels sand loosely all around with her front flippers in order to hide the nest from predators.

Exhausted from the effort, she slowly creeps back

The exhaustion of laying more than 100 eggs seems to show on the face of this mother sea turtle. **Opposite:** *The female scoops out a nest for her eggs.*

down the beach and slides into the sea. She might return in another fifteen days to lay another clutch of eggs within a few hundred yards of where she had laid tonight's nest. Then she might not return for several years.

Researchers don't know how sea turtles find their way back to the same beaches where they hatched as long as fifty years before. They believe that they may follow cues such as smells, ocean currents, Earth's magnetic field, or the sound of the surf on the beach. Other scientists think perhaps first-time mothers follow experienced females to their favorite nesting sites.

Above: *How sea turtles return to where they were born is still something of a mystery.*
Opposite: *A mother sea turtle returning to the sea after laying her eggs*

CHAPTER FOUR

Time in the Sea

Scientists can give you minute-by-minute accounts of a mother sea turtle's activities on land, but once she returns to the sea, most of her life and that of her young remain a mystery. Scientists have only a vague idea about where baby sea turtles go.

Once they have made it to the water's edge, the newly hatched sea turtles swim continuously for twenty-four or forty-eight hours until they have escaped the dangers of their birthplace. How do they know which way to swim? At first they swim into the waves. As they move into deeper water, the hatchlings switch to an internal magnetic compass. Biologists believe sea turtles can sense the angle and intensity of Earth's magnetic field. They are swept along by ocean currents until they reach areas where the currents converge.

Scientists believe that young sea turtles spend their early lives (researchers call it the "lost years") drifting in the open sea, often hiding and feeding in floating seaweed. Although hatchling-sized turtles have been seen in the Sargasso Sea, no one has yet discovered where most baby sea turtles spend their childhood.

No one even knows how long this period lasts, although estimates range from three to seven years. Once they reach the size of a dinner plate, fewer other animals can eat them, and the young turtles may dare to come closer to land.

Sea turtles take between ten and fifty years, depending on the species, to reach the age when they can reproduce. It's hard to tell the age of a sea turtle, because you can't count the rings on a sea turtle as you can on a tree (or even on a fish) to find out exactly how old it is. Captive sea turtles in aquariums—where there's plenty of food and no predators—often live much longer than sea turtles in the wild.

TURTLE TAG— A GAME SCIENTISTS PLAY

What scientists do know about the lives of sea turtles in the ocean has come mostly from tagging them. Researchers began tagging turtles with metal tags about fifty years ago. Today, they also use high-tech

Opposite: *No one knows exactly where baby sea turtles, such as this newborn hawksbill, spend their early years.*

CAN YOU TELL HOW OLD I AM?

To find out how old a tree is, a forest ranger cuts down the tree and counts the number of rings on the trunk. Each ring represents one year of growth. You can also count the growth rings on the ear bone (otolith) of a fish. But for some creatures you can only guess how old they are.

satellite tags. Scientists glue radio transmitters to the shells of sea turtles, which enable the marine animals to be tracked by satellites. Every time a radio-tagged sea turtle surfaces to breathe, the antenna on its back sends a signal to a satellite 22,000 miles above it. The signals pinpoint its location, its migration path, and how long it stays underwater (in Kemp's ridley turtles, 96 percent of the time).

Some high-tech tags are placed inside the turtles. PIT tags (for *Passive Integrated Transponder*) were implanted into the shoulder muscles of leatherback turtles. These turtles, caught off the coast of Nova Scotia, were released back into the sea carrying bar codes like the ones used to price groceries at the checkout-counter scanners. The tags let researchers identify each turtle individually. The only problem is that scientists have to be able to get close enough to scan the tag.

Stephen Morreale and a team of researchers from Cornell University tracked eight tagged leatherback sea turtles for up to three months at a time over the course of three years. They found that all eight used the same route to migrate from nesting sites in Costa Rica in Central America across the Pacific Ocean to the Galápagos Islands. (Other, longer studies of sea-turtle migrations, however, showed that sea turtles may vary their paths somewhat.)

Scientists suspect these long-distance travelers fol-

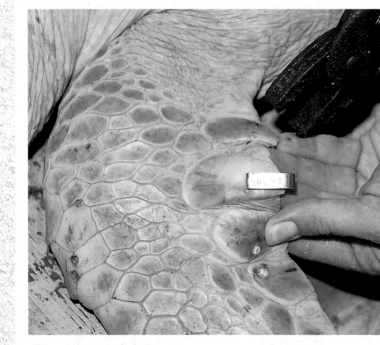

Above: *Scientists tag sea turtles to learn about their migrations.*
Opposite: *Students measure a loggerhead turtle caught for tagging.*

Scientist and children weigh and measure a hawksbill at the Underwater Observatory Marine Park in Eilat, Israel.

places, all the turtles that hatched on a particular beach over the years should share similar and distinctive DNA. To his surprise, Brian found that about half the turtles feeding in the Mediterranean Sea in Europe came from U.S. beaches. Even though they return to the place they were born to lay their eggs, sea turtles travel far and wide in search of food. This

low navigational cues, such as the length of daylight and Earth's magnetic field (like an internal compass). If we knew their migratory routes, we might be able to reroute boat traffic to prevent collisions between fishing boats and sea turtles.

Another way to track sea turtles is by *genetic tagging*. Brian Bowen and other biologists took blood samples from young loggerhead sea turtles feeding in a lagoon in Baja, Mexico. They compared the kind of DNA that they get only from their mothers with other turtles to trace these hatchlings' relatives. Because mother turtles return to their own birth-

Scientists from the University of Central Florida take blood samples to find out about a turtle's DNA.

research provides an important lesson for sea-turtle conservation: Because sea turtles travel worldwide, no single country alone can protect them.

CHAPTER FIVE

Is Time Running Out?

Some people fear that sea turtles are going the way of the dinosaurs. After having outlived them by sixty-five million years, sea turtles are now teetering on the edge of extinction. All eight species of sea turtles are listed as endangered or threatened, which means their populations are greatly reduced.

Although a mother sea turtle may lay several batches of a hundred or more eggs each time she breeds, she usually doesn't begin reproducing until she is about twenty-five years old, and some turtles don't have their first babies until they are almost fifty! Because it takes so long for a sea turtle to mature, it also takes a long time to replace a population that's been depleted by fishing, pollution, or other causes.

WHAT IS KILLING THE SEA TURTLES?

In the days of sail, seafarers traveling through tropical waters often captured female sea turtles as they struggled up the beaches to lay their eggs. They stored the living turtles on their backs in the holds of the ships. (Although turning it on its back made it impossible for a turtle to escape, it did help the turtle to breathe more easily out of water by relieving the weight of its shell on its lungs.) When fresh meat was needed on a long voyage, a turtle was brought on deck and slaughtered. The demand for sea-turtle soup—a popular food fad in London in the 1800s—and tortoiseshell combs also motivated sailors to return with a ship full of turtles.

Tropical islanders have long regarded turtle eggs as a delicacy. In fact, turtle eggs were once used to pay rent to the local ruler, the sultan of Sulu, in Southeast Asia. Poaching eggs for food or their supposed medicinal power has devastated many sea-turtle populations.

In some places, female turtles can no longer get to

the beaches where they had hatched in order to lay their eggs. Or if they do, their former homes are unrecognizable. Their nesting sites have been replaced or blocked by hotels, condominiums, and seawalls. Even where beaches remain, females may not come ashore, disoriented by tall buildings or the unfamiliar scent of sand trucked in to fill eroding beaches. If they do lay eggs, their hatchlings, confused by streetlights and car lights, may head toward land instead of the sea. In addition to human-caused problems, natural disasters, such as hurricanes, can flood beaches and wash eggs out of their nests.

In the open ocean, pollution and fishing nets are the turtles' greatest dangers. Nondegradable garbage such as balloons, plastic bottles, and plastic bags are often mistaken for jellyfish, and sea turtles can become entangled in fishing nets or cast-off rope or fishing line. The biggest threat is the shrimp trawl. It is a heavy net that is dragged along the ocean floor, scooping up everything in its path. Shrimp fishermen throw back about four-fifths of what they catch. The discards may be young fish, crabs, lobsters, or sea turtles. Most are dead by the time the nets are hauled onto the boats.

Another danger to sea turtles comes from a type of fishing gear that catches tuna, swordfish, and other large fish. Fishermen known as long-liners set strings of fishing lines baited with as many as two thousand hooks, leaving them to drift with the currents. These longlines sometimes stretch across thirty miles of ocean. Glow-in-the-dark light sticks are hung on the fishing lines to lure tuna and swordfish to the hooks. They also attract leatherback sea turtles, which apparently mistake them for jellyfish.

Many turtles are caught and drowned by fishing gear.

WHO IS HELPING TO SAVE THE TURTLES?

Community conservation, in which everyone has a stake in saving the turtles, is one of the best ways to ensure that sea turtles survive. In parts of Brazil,

32

Central America, and Southeast Asia, sea turtles were once only a source of delicious meat and valued eggs. Now, with conservationists and local residents working together, whole villages have turned from poaching eggs to protecting sea-turtle nesting sites. Some residents are paid to patrol the beaches to guard against poaching by humans or by wild animals. If the nests are in danger, game wardens may dig up the eggs and rebury them in protected hatcheries. Hunters who once raided nests now guide tourists to see these appealing animals lay their eggs. Villagers have discovered that sea turtles are more valuable alive than dead, not just to the environment but also to the local economy.

In many places, fishermen have been responsible for the decline of local sea-turtle populations, but in Nova Scotia, fishermen are working with scientists to track turtle migration to help rebuild the population. As leatherback sea turtles swim past their coast between June and August, fishermen call in turtle sightings from their fishing vessels. If they can get close enough, they photograph the giant beasts as they swim by. Distinctive markings on the turtles' heads help the researchers track individual animals. By providing a glimpse into part of the leatherbacks' lives, more than a hundred fishermen are helping to gather information that will be used to develop conservation plans for these endangered animals.

One of the greatest threats to sea turtles comes from shrimping boats. Often sea turtles are caught in nets along with the schools of shrimp; by the time the nets are raised to the surface, the air-breathing turtles have drowned. *Turtle Excluder Devices* (TEDs) are now required on all U.S. shrimp-fishing boats. A turtle excluder device is a slanted metal chute that is sewn into the end of a shrimp net. It has a trapdoor that allows the animals to slip out of the net before they drown. Scientists estimate that TEDs make it possible for 97 percent of the sea turtles to escape while keeping most of the shrimp (too small to open the door) in the net. Fishermen worry that some of their shrimp catch escapes through the turtle excluder devices, but without them, an estimated 55,000 sea turtles would be caught and drowned each year. Turtle excluder devices also reduce the catch of other unwanted animals.

Countries like the United States, Brazil, and India are making progress in protecting sea turtles, and recently there has been an upturn in the populations of loggerheads and olive ridleys. But individual countries can't do it alone. As we learn just how far sea turtles migrate, the need for international cooperation to protect sea turtles becomes even more urgent.

While many countries agree that it is important to protect endangered species, when it comes to taking action, it's a lot harder to find cooperation. Of the seventy-five countries that supply shrimp to U.S. markets, only twelve have laws requiring the use of turtle excluder devices, and even they don't check to make sure their fishermen comply with the laws. The United States reserves the right to ban shrimp imports from countries that don't require TEDs.

Local efforts may make the most difference. In Florida, which has over 90 percent of all sea-turtle nesting sites in North America, many residents make sure their guests from the sea feel welcome. Some towns in Florida require that waterfront residents and hotels dim their lights or turn them off during turtle nesting season. Other communities require that shields be put up on the ocean-facing side of street lamps and other lights. One conservation group in Florida went to court to block a plan a town had approved to build seawalls that would have cut off a favorite turtle nesting site.

People are using their buying power as consumers to change the way fishermen and fish dealers operate. In 1990, the public demand for dolphin-safe tuna forced tuna harvesters to change the way they catch tuna. Now some people are organizing a campaign to guarantee that shrimp fishermen use TEDs. In San Francisco and in Boston, and perhaps soon in other cities, some fish dealers are selling "turtle-friendly" shrimp, guaranteeing that they were caught in nets outfitted with turtle excluder devices. When you go

All of us can help protect sea turtles.

into a restaurant and order shrimp, you might ask, "Is it turtle-safe?"

Sea turtles also need more refuges. The coastal

waters where sea turtles gather to mate should be restricted from fishing during breeding season. Mother turtles also need safe havens where they can lay their eggs without being disturbed by poachers, bright lights, or even well-meaning tourists who flock to the beach to witness this miracle of nature and instead scare away the nesting turtles.

More research is needed to learn if there are regular migration routes that sea turtles use to travel between their feeding grounds and their nesting beaches. If there are, and if tagging studies can show where these routes are, then perhaps governments could ban fishing in these areas when the turtles are passing through.

These children are feeding lettuce to a green sea turtle.

SEA-TURTLE HOSPITALS

Sea-turtle hospitals treat stranded, sick, and wounded sea turtles. Each fall, a sea-turtle rehabilitation center at the New England Aquarium in Boston treats cold-stunned turtles that had wandered into the shallow waters of Cape Cod Bay during the warm summer months and waited too long to leave. A sudden cold snap in late autumn may strand hundreds of young sea turtles. Common symptoms of cold-stunned turtles, says Connie Merigo, Stranding Program coordinator, are frostbitten eyes and the tips of the flippers. As in a hospital, the Stranding Program workers, many of them volunteers, use fetal heart monitors to check their patients' pulse, X rays to diagnose cases of pneumonia, and CAT scans and blood samples to find out what other complications the sick turtles may have. Another turtle hospital on the Florida Keys operates on sick turtles to remove tumors and obstructions. They keep the turtles in outdoor pools until they are well enough to return to the ocean.

Sea-turtle hospitals help sea turtles that have swallowed fishhooks or been cold-stunned, wounded by sharks, struck by boats, or entangled in fishing nets. Some need waterproof casts to repair broken shells or flippers. When the turtles are

well again, they are tagged and released into the ocean. Sea-turtle rehabilitation is fairly new, so each new case adds to researchers' knowledge about turtle health.

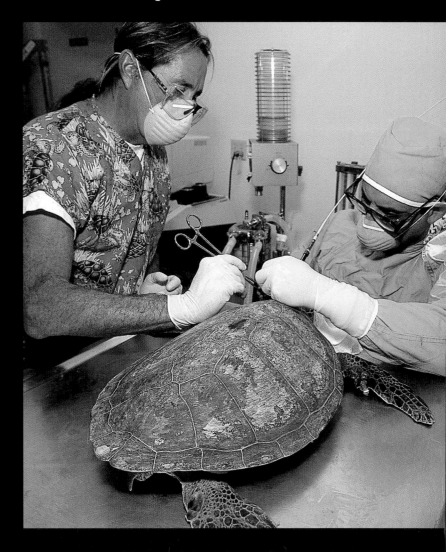

State-of-the-art turtle hospitals treat ailing sea turtles.

All that people are learning about sea turtles is being used to rescue them, not only from fishing nets and disease, but from extinction itself. At the Underwater Observatory Marine Park in Eilat, Israel, Curator Guy Ayalon and his staff have hatched, raised, and released 120 hawksbill sea turtles. He says, "There are important reasons for doing this project. First, hawksbill turtles are in danger of extinction. Second, in nature, more than 90 percent of sea turtles die at a young age. This is the reason that it is so important for us to raise them here at the park for nine months before releasing them to the sea. This project is done in cooperation with the community of Eilat and with the involvement of the local school-children, which naturally leads to their being more conscious of nature conservation and the need to protect the ocean environment, especially the sea turtles."

Other sea-turtle rescue programs assert that sea-turtle populations can better be served by protecting nesting beaches and reducing deaths of adult turtles at the hands of poachers and fishermen. But the intent of all these efforts is the same—to ensure that sea turtles, the original ocean nomads, are welcome wherever they roam.

ONE PERSON WHO MADE A DIFFERENCE

If sea turtles have a best friend, it is Dr. Archie Carr. He was a wildlife biologist who spent a lifetime learning, teaching, and writing about sea turtles. He also worked to preserve and protect sea turtles around the world, and inspired others to do the same. Dr. Carr helped establish national parks to preserve sea-turtle nesting sites. His warnings about the collapse of sea-turtle populations from habitat destruction and overfishing led to the formation of the Caribbean Conservation Corporation to push for the protection of sea turtles. After his death in 1987, Congress established the Archie Carr National Wildlife Refuge to protect a twenty-mile stretch of beach along Florida's east coast where loggerhead, green, and occasionally leatherback turtles come to lay their eggs.

Archie Carr devoted fifty-five years to the study of sea turtles, and he knew more about them than any other person. When Dr. Carr died, an admirer wrote of him: "His work with sea turtles taught him to see the world as few people have—through the eyes of other species."

WHAT CAN ONE PERSON DO?

Find out about organizations that are working to protect sea turtles and share what you learn.
You could start with these groups or look up "sea turtles" on the Internet:

Caribbean Conservation Corporation

4424 NW 13th St., Suite #1A

Gainesville, FL 32609

www.cccturtle.org

Center for Marine Conservation

1725 DeSales Street, NW, Suite 600

Washington, DC 20036

www.cmc-ocean.org

- Help keep the sea turtles' home clean. Take part in a beach cleanup and encourage recycling at home and at school. By cutting down on garbage, fertilizers, gasoline, and cleaning products, you reduce the amount of harmful chemicals and wastes that can end up in our water and eventually make their way into the ocean.

- Instead of releasing helium balloons, celebrate by releasing dragonflies or ladybugs (available from biological supply catalogs), which will also help the environment.

- Be a savvy consumer. Ask for turtle-safe seafood. Don't buy real tortoiseshell jewelry or ornaments.

- Write letters to politicians supporting turtle-protection laws.

- "Adopt" a turtle to support sea-turtle research and conservation.

- Take a "turtle walk." Should you have the opportunity to accompany a responsible guide to see a sea turtle lay her eggs on the beach at night, it will be a drama you will never forget. The money raised by these walks often helps support sea-turtle rescue and rehabilitation projects. (In Florida, the nesting season for sea turtles runs from May through October.)

GLOSSARY

ARRIBADA • A mass nesting of sea turtles

CARAPACE • The top shell of a turtle, an outgrowth of bone

COLD-BLOODED • Having a body temperature that changes with the surrounding air or water. Most fish, amphibians, and reptiles are cold-blooded.

DNA • Deoxyribonucleic acid (DNA) is a complex chemical found in all living things. It passes on all the information needed for cells to copy themselves and for a plant, animal, or even bacteria to pass on the characteristics of the parents to their children.

HATCHLING • Newly hatched, baby sea turtle

Hz • Hertz, which is a unit of frequency as it relates to sound

LONG-LINING • The fishing method in which strings of fishing lines baited with as many as 2,000 hooks are left to drift with the currents

LOST YEARS • A term used to refer to the years between a turtle's hatching and its return to coastal waters as a juvenile

PLASTRON • The bony plate that forms the turtle's bottom shell, covering its belly

REPTILE • A member of a class of cold-blooded animals with a backbone, usually having scales. Includes snakes, lizards, crocodiles, and turtles

SCUTES • The scales that cover the shell of a turtle, made of keratin (like your fingernails)

TURTLE EXCLUDER DEVICE (TED) • A release hatch placed in a trawler net that allows sea turtles to escape before they are drowned, while retaining the desired catch

BIBLIOGRAPHY

Ancona, George. *Turtle Watch.* New York: Macmillan Publishers, 1987.

Carr, Archie. *So Excellent a Fishe: A Natural History of Sea Turtles.* Garden City, N.Y.: Natural History Press, 1967.

Earle, Sylvia A., and Henry Wolcott. *Wild Oceans: America's Parks Under the Sea.* Washington, D.C.: National Geographic Society, 1999.

Guiberson, Brenda Z. *Into the Sea.* New York: Henry Holt & Co., 1996.

Ripple, Jeff. *Sea Turtles.* Stillwater, MN: Voyageur Press, 1996.

Rudloe, Jack. *Time of the Turtle.* New York: Truman Talley Books, 1989.

INDEX

(Page numbers in *italics* indicate photographs.)